The New Ewart:
Poems 1980–1982

The New Ewart:
Poems 1980-1982

by Gavin Ewart

Hutchinson
London Sydney Melbourne Auckland Johannesburg

Hutchinson & Co. (Publishers) Ltd

An imprint of the Hutchinson Publishing Group

17–21 Conway Street, London W1P 5HL

Hutchinson Group (Australia) Pty Ltd
30–32 Cremorne Street, Richmond South, Victoria 3121
PO Box 151, Broadway, New South Wales 2007

Hutchinson Group (NZ) Ltd
32–34 View Road, PO Box 40–086, Glenfield, Auckland 10

Hutchinson Group (SA) Pty Ltd
PO Box 337, Bergvlei 2012, South Africa

First published 1982
© Gavin Ewart 1982

Set in VIP Bembo by
D. P. Media Limited, Hitchin, Hertfordshire

Printed in Great Britain by
The Anchor Press Ltd, and bound by
Wm Brendon & Son Ltd, both of Tiptree, Essex

ISBN 0 09 146980 5

For Lincoln Kirstein and Peter Porter
and in memory of Giles Romilly and John Madge

Bring out number, weight, and measure
in a year of dearth

Contents

PART THREE

PART FOUR

Acknowledgements

Some of the poems in this book have appeared in *Ambit*, *Aquarius*, *Bananas*, *Encounter*, *Gallery*, *London Magazine*, *New Statesman*, *Nova*, *Poetry London*, *Poetry Review*, *Stand*, *Thames Poetry*, *The Honest Ulsterman*, *The Listener*, *The Times Literary Supplement*. Others have been included in the Arts Council anthology *New Poetry 4*, in the Poetry Section of the PEN Broadsheet edited by Fleur Adcock, in *Larkin at Sixty* published by Faber and Faber, and in the Poetry Book Society Supplement for Christmas 1980 edited by Peter Porter. Some have been broadcast by the BBC ('Not Now, I'm Listening' and 'Poetry Now'). The poem 'Gritty' was first published in *Chapter and Verse*, a pamphlet produced by the Mandeville Press.

PART ONE

The Wicked Uncle

Every prune-faced prissy straitlaced serious writer,
      as he sits with his goose quill in his ivory tower
      in the Land of Received Ideas, sipping Veuve Cliché,

dreams of that wicked uncle, the uninhibited natural
   man,
      down in the roaring bar drinking owl-tighteners,
      snapping the garters of the juicy serving wenches,

at home with the crude commercials, with statutory
   powers
      as a Philistine – whose tales of Art and Lance
      have nothing to do with Round Tables, Grails or
         Love.

Admired everywhere for his crude wit, one for the girls
      in every century, a gambler, irresponsible
      in a tweed suit, a prosperous Prospero,

numerate, in everything to do with golden shitlike
   money
      childishly an expert – simple music, simple jokes
      keep him happy, it's the Life Force surely

that pushes him up the board, a pawn of Freedom,
      the world his nursery, he is so enviable,
      so unlike his contemplative nephew, it's not true!

Exits

If you imagine life as a large room,
most of the Exits are marked Painful –
and this is what causes fear,
to get from here to there
the despot, the dandy and the duffer
all have to suffer.

But with the sudden atomic boom –
this is what makes some men disdainful
of death – or the slick quick knife
or shot, you're out of life
like that! bingo! couldn't be faster!
And that's no disaster.

It's when the slow darknesses loom,
the clouds look doom-laden and rainful,
the lightning hysterias fly
across the agonized sky.
Long illness brings dreams of funerals, hearses –
but sudden death: mercies.

Don't mourn them, like some stolid marble tomb,
those who go out like a light – gainful
it isn't, and they had luck,
missed what we all would duck
if we'd the choice: feeling iller and iller.
Long live the instant killer!

25A Norfolk Crescent

It's odd to think how
in that once-untenanted space
above our house
a man is having a bath,
a man and a woman are making love,
life is going on
in what once was air.

In that block of luxury flats
nobody knows now where
the nursery was;
it's so easy to blame
my father's 'I'm very disappointed in you'
for ambition
and the feeling lost.

Mother's comfort. Too much;
and in Cambridge Square
two twin boys
were learning to be queers.
'As the twig is bent', they say,
it's all written,
they say, or in the stars.

The intelligent children
understand the insults –
they suffer most.
The dim ones just grin.
If I had imagination – too much –
my father none,
that was my bad luck.

At this distance in time
the fear and hate exist
but can't be touched –
that house is now a ghost
within a house, where others now
live and suffer.
Tall in the anxious air.

Ode

'What the world needs are warmer hearts,
Not older poets.' – Auden and Kallman, *Elegy For Young
Lovers*

As wisdom percolates down
more slowly than water through coffee,
    our Progress may seem to be back –

    this century, three-quarters done,
has screamed *If you don't like it, kill it!*
    and millions are mute as result,

    in the water, the earth or the air
their particles rest or are wafted –
    are we much better off than before?

    Yet everything should be tried once,
aphoristic clichés are too tidy;
    when murder's a way that's been found

    no good, in the end, to win friends
and in general counter-productive,
    we might even try something else?

    No poet of sixty's a sage,
any more than a saxophone player,
    he can't say *Do this!* or *Do that!*,

    morals aren't his peculiar sphere,
his opinions are quite often silly.
    In an age when some writers can't read,

    so spontaneous it isn't true,
'gut reactions' get too freely mentioned –
    but it all must go in through the brain,

    no experience, none, can escape
when the senses flash messages light-speed
    or reporterlike telephone in.

There is hope, while the human brain works,
SF addicts may turn out false prophets.
    Selective or general culls

        on the basis of colour or class,
by rampageous and wicked religions,
    we might, in the end, quite avoid.

    But the *heart*? Ah! Emotions so far,
as they sulk or play tag in the sunshine,
    have been quite an unbiddable lot –

    they *'won't* be told', that is the phrase,
or ordered about, they're haphazard,
    and they want some improbable things.

    Proud ladies in big flowery hats
dream of being held down, naked, and peed on
    by the whole of a rugger fifteen.

    Fantasies of such kinds are not rare
when the hormones, at home with the feelings,
    drink too much of our social champagne.

    As with weather, to forecast or hope
that our hearts grow perceptibly warmer
    is more or less all we can do –

    not giving up hope is the thing,
in the old-fashioned phrase, to be sanguine
    is the must for us creatures of blood.

Invitations

Invitations aren't easy.
When I was in my early twenties
I was giving a party.
I wanted to ask one friend – but not his wife.
My mother said: 'You must ask them both.'
But I was very loth!

She made me feel queasy.
Was she exactly *compos mentis*?
Oh, she shone like a Smartie
but I didn't want her – not on your life!
Now I know that it's not a party that one gives –
but drinks to relatives.

You can't leave out Josie
or really terrible Freddy
who's the boyfriend of a cousin,
your husband's family are all lining up.
There's something about the words *in-law*
that sticks in your craw.

It won't be very cosy,
but you must be ready
to take on at least a dozen
you'd not be seen dead with – let alone wine, dine or sup!
He has to be fond of parasites, that one who suffers most,
so rightly called the host!

Dickens and I *

After reading in a Derbyshire school, the fifteen and the
sixteen-year-olds are clustering round me (no fool like an
old fool), the clevers, the athletics, the shys, the bolds,
for me to sign their poem-photostats. I write 'Best
wishes to Clare; John: Clive; Maureen'. These are their
souvenirs – Bard Rock, Hippocrene beer mats – xeroxed
to help them sort out what I mean, like worksheets. I'm
the only worksheet on the scene!

Behind me I feel pressure from the girls, the gentle touch
of blouses, sweaters, blazers; felt but not seen. But
something feminine swirls into my brain. Young eyes

* The prose of Dickens often contains iambic pentameters, unconsciously
admitted. In these instances it should be re-named: prerse or vose. This poem,
consciously, is made up of rhyming lines printed as prose.

clear as lasers. It's like the scent of roses from a bed
where, still unpruned, the roses, jostling, cluster and of
the senses only one is fed but that's enough to soothe the
sensual lustre – sex is that killing air, I tell you, buster!

But this is calm, I'm old. To jump about in goatlike joy is
something long gone by. Yet we have much in common,
there's no doubt, if you consider it – Dickens and I. He
came on Ellen Ternan crying backstage, a teenage girl
ashamed of wearing tights; he loved young women less
than half his age, he went round reading, liked his name
in lights. We'd be called tender, if we had our rights.

In the Restaurant

At the tables there is laughter, where executives are
    lunching.
'You're so beautiful!' a man says; there is holding hands
    (and footlove)
as the dishes and the egos, with experimental cooking,
so exaggerate the meetings and the matings of the
    twosomes.
All percentages and products are examined in the aura
of the wine carafes of redness that emblazon on the table
just the pinkness of the patches where white cloth is
    wobbled over –
as the sun that is our sovereign shines enticingly deep
    through them.

But the lovers and the agents, all of them demand a
    profit –
it may come in cheques, or simply the wet warmth of
    something fluffy.
For the laughter and the lovetalk are by no means, here,
    unselfish,
there is no one in the world who won't seek his own
    advantage
or seek hers (and I must say this); every altruistic action

19

is itself a conscience-soother and still has its private
   audience
of a God who sits in judgment, or more public
   approbation.
All the women stroke men's torsos for their own delight
   and sharing.

There's a two-way traffic running even in the kissing
   glances
of a girl who eyes a loved one over plates of fegatoni.
Even gold-diggers are giving, in a sense it's all a bargain.
See the black and busty hustle of the waitresses,
   good-natured
in the face of many orders; they are paid, of course, to do
   it.
It's so true we all want something – and that something
   might be someone –
that the only problem left is: do we do it sad, or gaily?
restaurants are no exception, and the whole of life is
   business.

The Big Hand

The big hand guides the hand to write an A,
the big hand guides the hand to write a B,
the big hand smacks the hand that writes a c
because all letters must be big letters,
only what is big can glorify the alphabet.

Small letters are shy and mean, the big hand knows,
they come out of hiding with what is coarse and
   common,
pinned to each day, knitted into each day,
eaten each day as so much necessary food.

The big letters are gods, they never eat or sleep
or clothe or copulate. Although they sound the same
they lie on paper in their pride of place –

20

anyone with eyes can see they're different.
The big hand made them in the time of giants,
there is no limit to their largeness,
they cavort in the sky, they rule the universe.

The little letters are like self-made men,
like men made out of stones, like useful ants
that swarm through letterpress; they never pretend to be
   big.
With them you can write loveletters or holy books
while the proud big letters are standing still in the sky.

Ballad

The kinky kisses
are near us in the night –
I cleared my brain of little girls
and tried to put it right.
The moon is bright.

The lurid lyrics
are sung beneath one's breath –
I put in gaol my dear desires
and sentenced them to death,
Elizabeth.

The naughty knifelets
shine with a sheen that kills –
I hospitalized my violence
and gave them sleeping pills.
The night wind chills.

The sexy singles
sell well in porno shops –
I dramatized my impulses
and told them they were flops.
The dark owl drops.

The randy razors
glint on, into my dream –
this one I cherish specially,
as you, perhaps, ice cream.
Oh, please, don't scream!

The blood runs blackly
under the blade's caress –
her life just hesitates away,
a shy girl to undress.
Oh, happiness!

The Semi-Sapphics

Oh no! Alcoholics don't dwindle into a happy twilight
like a permanent saloon bar between the wars, like
     something
beautifully written by old egghead P.G. Wodehouse –
          Mulliner's mildness

scouting for narrative, when a Large Gin and Tonic
tells a Small Brown Ale how it loved a girl and lost her
among the old beans and the aunts, where Lord
     Emsworth,
          the Efficient Baxter

and a loony doctor or two are the worst things you'd
     meet with.
Sociable, of course, the bars are – but also phoney
and the lonely women find disgusting faces on the
     pillows,
          waking next morning

with their simply putrid pick-ups from last night's
     drinking.
They are The Lost Girls (and Jean Rhys understood
     them),
the ones who have to live with only bottles for comfort –
          nobody loves them.

The Church is cold, perhaps, and very much less sexy,
but at least in physical terms it doesn't poison you.
It would be nice to say that, but of course you can't, of the
    Alehouse.
            Warm but waspish,

it has a sting in its tail; and the hung-over horrors
lead on to the hairs of the dog that bit them,
when they feel fragile and fear they are frigid,
            most unattractive.

Looking at mirrors never makes them feel much better.
The best you can wish them is someone to like them,
the frank confidence, the reciprocated cuddle.
            That might improve them.

War Death in a Low Key

This all happened in 1943, near Algiers.
I was at a base camp, waiting to be posted,
a Second Lieutenant in a Light Anti-Aircraft Regiment –
but my unit had dumped me (for a more efficient
    officer),
following an exercise where my map-reading had been
    faulty
(the maps were fairly old).
I had to start the whole thing. I had to lead the Troop off
and the road I was on wasn't even on the map;
consequently I took the wrong turning at the wrong
    crossroads.
'Understandable, but inexcusable,' the Assessor said
    later.

It was hot as hell. There was a donkey in the camp that
    brayed all day long,
a depressing sound. I was depressed, and felt like a reject.
There was a Captain with alopecia from the Eighth
    Army,

who wore his black beret all the time and made a very big
    thing
about being a Desert Rat (we, of course, were First
    Army) –
the war in North Africa was very nearly over
and the Germans and Italians were about to be pushed off
    Cape Bon
into the sea. This Captain was by way of being
a hand grenade instructor. Some of these junior officers
obviously worshipped him because of his daring,
and they would lob grenades about among each other.
One subaltern, one day, lobbed (or held) one once too
    often.
The top of his head was blown off, though his rimless
    glasses
stayed on his nose. Panic on the range.

I was told all this at lunchtime.
Later (because I'd known him? But I
hadn't really. I just knew which he was)
I was detailed to be part of the Guard of Honour at his
    funeral.

How many were there? Three or four of us? And the
    driver.
His body lay on a stretcher on the floor
of an open 15 cwt. We collected it from the Hospital.
There was no coffin. He was wrapped tight in a
grey army blanket (as I remember). Blood still oozed
    through
at the top, where his head was.
Over-awed, I think, we sat in the truck with our rifles.

There was another burial, I remember.
A woman, a nursing sister. No coffin either.
She was wrapped from head to toe in bandages
like a rather plump, short mummy.
Somehow it was pathetic to see the mound of her breasts
and realize it was a woman. Young men's reactions
to such things are usually quite other.

24

The prayers were said, the red soil scattered on.
We fired, together, our valedictory volley.

We were quiet, but relieved, as we drove home empty.
His name began with an A? It's hard, now, to remember.
Someone that night slightly shocked me by saying:
'I knew him – but I'm afraid I didn't like him.'

Sestina: The Literary Gathering

At one end of the peculiar table Jeremy
sat, and talked about poetry to Carl.
He was a bit of a nutter. Next to him, Sheila
was eating a farinaceous dish. Lewis
listened intently to the words of Ursula.
They were all drinking cider. And so was Jane.

There was something quiet and achieved about Jane –
of course she was a good deal older than Lewis –
and she hadn't got the manic quality of Jeremy
nor did she understand engineering, like Carl,
or the details of catering, which obviously Ursula
had at her fingertips. They all liked Sheila.

They all agreed there was no one like Sheila
for lovability. Music to Jeremy
was the breath of life. Often, to Carl,
he would play his autoharp – this delighted Ursula
and certainly caused some pleasure to Jane –
sitting in the meadow with the cows and Lewis.

'Lewis?' said Jane. 'He's a dark horse, Lewis!'
'You never know what he's thinking!' cried Sheila.
'He's a very nice boy' was the verdict of Ursula;
he seemed more ordinary to Carl and Jeremy.
He was fond of Milton (he once told Jane) –
but only modern poets appealed to Carl.

There was a hint of dark Satanic mills about Carl,
a contained intelligence; no fly-by-night Jeremy, he
hadn't the open character of Ursula,
in this respect he was more like Jane
or the sheep and the cattle. And only Sheila
seemed to understand him – except for Ursula.

There was a bardic bravery about Ursula.
Not even Lewis, or Jane, or Sheila
had her bravura – in the words of Lewis
'She is the mother of us all!' For Jane
Ursula's writing was the tops, and Carl
confessed he was staggered, and even Jeremy,

though he liked Carl and respected Jane
and admired Lewis (and the work of Sheila),
said how he, Jeremy, really worshipped Ursula.

Circe I

Her Caliban cunt
was wild and woolly,
her nipples like
the ends of lemons,
she was an expert on
all kinds of pigfood.

For the rough sailors
she poured the wine out,
but for one man only
she plumped satin cushions,
spreading her bum,
inviting him in.

He felt so special,
a wonderful lover,
superior grunting
in bowers of vine-leaves;
pigs their background
and love their pigfood.

26

Circe II

It certainly is the smell of her cunt
makes you fall on your knees and grunt.

It certainly is the slope of her tits
makes your morality fall to bits.

It certainly is her incurved waist
makes you long for that truffle taste.

It certainly is her pubic thighs
makes your piglike prick uprise.

It certainly is her heavenly hair
makes you wallow and keeps you bare.

It certainly is her beautiful bum
makes you rootle and holds you dumb.

It certainly is her feminine hands
makes you the slave of glorious glands.

It certainly is the commanding eye
makes you happy to live in a sty.

Every Doggerel has its Day

The sun winks back from the back of the blade – John Arlott,
BBC commentary on the Second Test Match, England
v. Australia, 11 July 1977

The sun winks back from the back of the blade,
the commentators sit in the shade
and, however many runs are made,

it's a funny old game – sentimental too,
a ritual practised for me and you –
and Youth is the cause of the hullabaloo.

When the arm is strong and the eye is keen
the idea of old age is quite obscene.
But the County Cap (and the might-have-been)

lose the throwing arm and the timing sense,
however clever, however dense,
and the past, at last, is the only tense –

even the legendary W.G. Grace
at the very end couldn't stand the pace.
He vanished too – though not without trace –

and even a batsman as great as Hobbs
when he lay dead couldn't handle lobs –
this is what causes our sighs and sobs.

Old men with MCC-striped ties
lament lost vigour with watery eyes –
the active stroking of balls (and thighs).

Cricket for them's an escape from Life,
the worries of business, children, wife;
as Death stands by with his surgeon's knife

each fancies himself as a Peter Pan,
a young attractive cricketing man,
one of the fastest who ever ran

between the wickets or in to bowl,
a batsman with genius to lift the soul,
a merrier hitter than Old King Cole.

The game, as they sit and watch for hours,
reminds them of their longlost powers
until it's over – and *Send No Flowers*.

'Ce Petit Détail, Tellement Sexuel'

– Romain Rolland, *Le Six Octobre*

In the old days you were seriously worshipped,
carved on temples, always a prominent feature
of certain gods in gardens, propped in an upright position
on dead bodies of the Pharaohs;

secretly, the obelisks all celebrated you –
even the Victorians in Kensington Gardens
with the Speke Memorial obliquely remembered you –
and the spires of all the churches.

Jocular and lewd you exist at Pompeii
along with the scales and the Roman soldier
and all through the South small facsimiles of you
keep the Evil Eye from harming,

an Italian under-culture; and it's not surprising
that the word 'fascinate' (which belonged to the witches)
in the Greek and the Latin had its first meaning:
render impotent. Late Horace

used *fascinum* to mean you. You remain worrying
to all Puritans, and you can really frighten
bossy middle-aged busybodies. Like Armageddon,
truthfully they fear to see you.

Some religions impose a strict taboo
as rigid and inflexible as yourself; and detailed
representation in works of art, illegal,
is almost everywhere forbidden.

This is the bad news. There's a lot of it –
but I bring you too a modified message of hope.
As long as we exist, I think, in secret
your cult, enthusiastic twosomes

bowing down before you (as they always did),
will prosper; for the worshipping millions
in a real sense still owe their existence to you –
not quite a god, but a bold symbol.

Hunting the Badger by Owl-Light

The Elizabethans went stabbed to their death-boxes,
boys on stage squeaked like the Death's Head chrysalis,
gibbets like bus-stops in a land of death.

This was the start of something, life was death.
In deathly reverence divines like paper bags
exploded in sermons; *Death News* on every stand.

Death was a travel agent, crossing the Styx
was what the stoics fancied – the popular Death Special
was the Magical Mystery Tour the death-fanciers liked.

The Jokes of Early Aviation

The jokes of early aviation
were all about joysticks and cockpits –
the wartime ones, that rocked the aircrews,
were about pressing tits
and airscrews –

mechanical, verbal fornication,
and light relief for tomcat tomfools,
for dirty Dick and handsome Harry
(never, though good with tools,
would marry) –

as Mars, the god of masturbation,
held thousands there earthbound and grounded,
they praised with voices, not with bodies,
and seldom in a bed,
a Goddess.

30

In the Ninetieth Year

As my mother was dying
her head became skull-like,
her flesh left her bones.
She became more and more
like the skeletons they dig up,
curled, in hot countries.

Still alive, she was sleeping
more and more bone-like,
her heart's pounded thump
was all that distinguished her
from pre-history's burials,
the caves and the barrows.

Old bones are so neutral
and not really manlike,
for thought goes with flesh,
its lusts and its jealousies –
lose blood, and you're losing
the stuff of existence.

Cowardice *

Do you remember, in the Twenties,
the songs we used to sing,
reading our Westermans and Hentys,
before the days of Bing?
Gramophones were very sharp and tinny,
we could sit there and applaud
shows with stars like Laddie, Sonnie, Binnie,
Jack and Jessie, June and Claude.
We had no truck with opus numbers
or anything called Art –
and fox-trots (long before the rumbas)
gave us our happy start. . . .

This was our taste/ of the future,
we embraced/ that decade,
gleaming in glamour, with our hope not betrayed.
There lay Love – which our ten-year-old scoffing
felt above (girls with men!) – in the offing.

The sight of women set us giggling,
their bottoms broad and fat,
the Charleston and that sexy wriggling,
their bosoms not so flat,
as they jumped and bumped in that gay chorus –
though we watched the dance with scorn,
this was Life cavorting there before us,
and the reason we were born.
Of this we were just dimly conscious,
uneasily we'd sit
and judge, severe, like monks with tonsures –
soon to be part of it. . . .

It was all necks/ with arms round them,
grown-up sex/ on display –
a mystery coming our way.
We weren't too frightened,
we felt partly enlightened
in that faced-by-the-future far decade.

* Based on 'Dear Little Café', from Noël Coward's *Bitter Sweet*.
In 1926 (for the record) I was ten years old.

An Old Husband Suspects Adultery

I was just beginning to feel in the mood,
my desire was just beginning to harden,
as we lay cuddling like Babes in the Wood
or Adam and Eve naked in that Garden –
when the telephone started ringing.
She jumped out of bed (like Eve, naked)
and answered it – I could hear him darlinging.

She spoke to him coolly but she wasn't rude,
taking it in her stride with her long legs – flustered
she certainly wasn't. No thought of Bad or Good
grazed her. Domestic as custard
she talked, as if to a grocer,
like smooth-limbed Eve with a handset, naked,
standing there beautiful. I was feeling moroser

than I can tell you. A pin-up, a nude,
she'd made herself. Unreachable. She hung up
and climbed back into bed. Like Robin Hood
he'd robbed the rich – before he'd rung up
I'd really felt like doing it,
but now the thread was lost – Eve, so naked, couldn't
tempt me now into pursuing it.

Love Song

As you get old you begin to wonder –
what was all that lightning and thunder
actually about?
It was more than holding hands,
it had a lot to do with glands –
but now you're far out,

floating calmly in a lonely seascape;
passionate rose-garden, stormed treescape
very long ago
left behind – what they call Youth
seems now ridiculous, uncouth
(if you want to know).

As you settle into peace, or dourness,
that bitter-sweet, that sweet-and-sourness,
is a vanished taste;
yet those who never clasped and kissed
don't know exactly what they missed
or what went to waste.

Afrokill

1
The striped horse
is red inside
like sliced cake
There should be a notice
LIONS AT WORK

2
Pudgy plush muzzles
of faded yellow
of teddy-bear
show pinkness
from blood-nuzzle

3
They roll over
on invisible
beds, armchairs, divans,
sleeping so
foodful

4
The demon-faced
square pack-dogs
laugh at the banquet
brown snarling
lackeys

5
Last come the hopping
horrors
with big wings,
clean wavebreak
on shipwreck ribs.

Back

They come back, the terrible old words,
words like 'heart-piercing',
from the bad poems in the anthologies,
when I hear the voices of the children playing –
but not what they are saying.

I think back, ten or eleven years,
when we could hear sing
our own kids' trebles – the tree of knowledge is
apt to grow too fast in any London garden –
and soon our feelings harden.

They float back, like an archaic rhyme,
brightly transpiercing
parental minds, strong as old theologies,
sweet, that all too soon will grow both sour and flatter –
what they're saying doesn't matter.

MacNeice in Belfast 1938

Among the cranes and derricks
Herrick's verse seems odd,
and gantry, gull and gannet
span it, much as though God
(the poor old sod)
had gone off in hysterics.

A town hard, harsh, satiric.
Lyrics are out of place –
the only thing that's frisky,
whisky; whose golden face
shines through disgrace
and living that's empiric.

In many ways Satanic,
manic, and short of hope;
Noah might be left remaining.
Raining? Well, he could cope.
For Art, no scope.
But not much sign of panic.

A Contemporary Film of Lancasters in Action

To see them bombing up
and wheeling off into the dusk,
nose to tail, queueing, turning for the take-off,
like long-jumpers each one coming up
stationary
before they begin the run before the jump,
piloted by volunteer bank clerks.
Is my emotion bogus or inflationary?

I was never a hero,
the shark's tooth, boar's tusk,
seeming less frightening than this kind of flying,
for all kinds of courage rated zero,
admiringly
I admit they did what I could never,
sleepwalkers showing a sleepless courage –
long flights to firework climax, untiringly.

Obstinate, I survive
and, writing in this summer musk,
I say they were the patient venturing lions
and I the mean dog that stayed alive;
we owe them
every valedictory mark of respect
(bravery's facing such boring dangers)
that we can possibly, too late, show them.

36

A 14-Year Old Convalescent Cat
in the Winter

I want him to have another living summer,
to lie in the sun and enjoy the *douceur de vivre* –
because the sun, like golden rum in a rummer,
is what makes an idle cat *un tout petit peu ivre* –

I want him to lie stretched out, contented,
revelling in the heat, his fur all dry and warm,
an Old Age Pensioner, retired, resented
by no one, and happinesses in a beelike swarm

to settle on him – postponed for another season
that last fated hateful journey to the vet
from which there is no return (and age the reason),
which must soon come – as I cannot forget.

Conversation Piece

I sit and hear my mother and my aunt
talking of dog-carts, of a century gone
I try to imagine (there are some who can't).
Their total age is 181.
Under the clothes, the bodies were the same
as those the striptease, shamelessly as cards,
deals to the watchers now. Just the same game
but played by different rules; *ripostes, on guards,*

masks of all sorts, the flirting with a fan,
a kind of fencing with an instinct. Who loved who
they had their ways of knowing, woman and man.
Something outside them told them what to do.
They weren't direct like us (are we direct?),
Victoria sat there like a monolith
but even nice girls knew what to expect,
how Zeus crept up on Leda in the myth –

without a visiting card, in fancy dress.
No lady left the house without her gloves.
Deafness makes meaning something they must guess,
arthritis stiffens Venus and her doves,
for four decades no lovemaking at all –
beauty was jolly, with a motoring veil.
There should be writing, writing on the wall:
All sex shall fail, but love shall never fail.

The Dwarf with Brass Teeth

*And the door closed, and the latch clicked, but the prince with
stars for his eyes and a new moon for his mouth didn't mind, for
he was young and strong, and though he wasn't handsome, he
had heard lots of doors close and click before this one, and didn't
feel at all frightened. But he would have been if he had known
who had closed the door. It was the Dwarf with brass teeth, who
was more dreadful than the most spotted of all things, and whose
ears were fixed on backwards.*

Even those who later become featured
as Success Stories, journalisted and preachered,
don't really have an easy time
as they grow to being a dollar from being a dime –

the fairy story Get Rich Quick is for the dreamers;
successful people can be mean, and schemers,
and to make a lot of dough
you must work at it, and be a hard-hearted so-and-so.

Those who make lots of money or you-name-it
are riding the tiger but can never tame it;
and the admired Great Lovers too
have to stop doing other things they'd like to do.

You must go at it monomaniac, whole-hearted,
know that you're bound to lose, before you've started,
and what you lose most is 'If . . .'
all the alternative lives you could lead before you're stiff.

The possibilities are fewer and fewer, as you get older
and the wind and summer sun strike that much colder.
When the door shuts in the vaults
you're shut in with your own limitations and faults.

Settling for less than the best is what is hardest –
hence God and the drugs and the fevered artist –
but for Madge, Maud, Kenneth, Keith,
for all of us, the Dwarf grins – with his sharp brass teeth.

The Death of W.S. Gilbert at Harrow Weald

Imagine that flat glassy lake in 1911,
a very Victorian part of the prosperous house
(architect: Norman Shaw),
a beautiful hot summer's day in 1911.

'The tiny island in the middle of the lake flames with
      azaleas. . . .
The water's edge is fringed with golden iris and
      forget-me-nots,
and beside the winding pathway there is white heather
      for good fortune.
It is all set in a greenwood carpeted with half-uncurled
      bracken ferns,
where the shadowy fading bluebells might be fancied to
      ring
a muffled peal from fairyland.'

Into that water steps the white foot of a lady
and then, perhaps more timidly, the white foot of
      another lady.
They wear commodious and decorous bathing
      garments.
The water is very cold.
One lady is the pupil of the other lady
on that hot summer's day in 1911.

Gilbert has had lunch at the Junior Carlton,
he is teaching the more mature lady to swim. He is 74.

'My pupil was a much better swimmer than I,
and soon outdistanced me. We were both unaware
that the lake was deep further out,
and presently she tried to touch bottom and found herself
out of her depth. She shrieked out,
"Oh, Miss Emery, I am drowning!" '

A heavy body plunges into the water
like an old bull, like the leader of the herd,
with the scrotum tightened by that cold lake of 1911.
He swims to her, shouts advice: 'Put your hands on my
    shoulders!'
She feels him sink under her. He doesn't come up.
She struggles to the bank, he is dead of heart failure.

Is there a moral for old men? *Don't fool about with ladies?*
But all the same it's good to die brave
on a beautiful hot summer's day in 1911.

A Lyric of Love

As warm as a wasp's nest,
as cold as a key,
that is the way,
that is the worrying way
you've been to me;

as hot as a headache,
indifferent as ice,
that's what you've been,
that's what you've boringly been –
nasty and nice;

as jealous as ginger,
as neutral as knees,
that's how you treat me,
teasingly trap me and treat me –
fry me or freeze.

F For

As we fancy what is feminine and fimbriate
(as a farrier's familiar with fenugreek),
we fall friendly to those famous femmes fatales
whose fellatio
felled Field-Marshals freely.

For the female face is fabulous and fortunate
(and is favouring festivities and festivals),
far from fisticuffs and fiercely fatal fights,
felicific, its
fascination's forceful.

All those female forms are fleshy and fructiferous
(for us femiphiles so fitting, febrifugal)
and so full of femineity we feel
fine as feoffees, both
fuglemen and fulgent.

Property

In romantic fiction (which is women's pornography)
the heroine's hand, as it dives into the young man's zip
(though this is never mentioned),
is searching for a wedding ring;
though the books don't deal in physiological geography
it's always implied that marriage is the greatest trip
(to the romantic boss, who's well-intentioned) –
this is the one and only thing.

After the tables for two and the dances and car-petting
nail him down, they seem to say, to a beautiful house
where *everything* is beautiful,
with Old Masters all over the walls,
with every new gadget and deep-pile wall-to-wall
    carpeting –
where the wife is a kind of bossy ferocious mouse
and far more houseproud than dutiful,
where highborn neighbours pay calls

in a permanent paradise of chic materialism
and the sperm is just to produce a little bundle of love.
The thing that counts is status.
It's like a sentimental tune,
old-fashioned music in a time of discords and serialism.
So I am moved when I see the other kind of love,
lovers who touch in public (they may well hate us),
poor but not infected, entirely immune.

The Late Eighties

        To her
I am a coloured blur,
    a just-heard voice,
    as she sits there –
she hasn't any choice.

        Life fades
like on-off hearing aids,
    and in her sleep
    the realler world
is dreaming, long and deep.

        This now
needs living through somehow,
    patience is all
    and the time left,
though slow, is surely small.

I touch
the body changed so much,
   she understands
   some tenderness
through bony arms and hands.

      Contact
is joining and a fact;
   we once were one,
   and touching's how
all lovemaking gets done.

Infatuations

It's standard in our gossip to say
'I just can't think what he sees in *her*'
or 'I can't think what she sees in *him*'
and women are usually the sayers
(love is their game, and they are the players),

men don't seem to speculate in that way.
But it's striking how this thought can occur
in a different form, when the chance is slim
that two who have once been lovers
will ever join again under, or on top of, the covers.

They meet as different people always, they
find they've lost the flattering romantic blur
that blazed so strongly – that light is dim.
They, almost, think 'What did I ever . . . ?'
but hesitate, from pride. Admit such thoughts? Oh,
   never.

Down There on a Visit

Going is not straight in that cumbersome country,
molehills thick as molecules impede the pedestrian,
as the calamitous clay clings to his clogs.

Sight is not good in that land of apparitions
where at the eye's side trees tremble tremendously.
He wakes with his clock-watchers rimmed running with
    rheum.

Touch has gone shapeless in sweat-stained shivering.
The wonderful wines and the beautiful beers
are far-retchingly repulsive to the pasteboard palate.

Hearing has become almost equally horrible,
loud lout noises bang on his head-box
rattling around like parched peas in his brain-pan.

As he goes he mistrusts the gauche guiding locals,
interpreting mischief as mind-warping malice;
he is badly disposed to all, all beauty and boar-hunting.

To the Puritans who are the Gods of This World

It needed Cain and Abel too,
The brothers Murder and Incite
                    – C.H. Sisson

A Masturbating Mildred you,
or Would-Be-Fornicating Fred,
        not dead
but dying (as we all are too) –
        no shame
attaches to that age-old game,

but some to you! I see you both
as too-genteel Victorian types
        with pipes,
a lively dread of that giant Sloth,
        no votes
and bonnets, bustles, petticoats –

the man and woman of it. Still
you won't admit such dangerous acts
        as facts.
On the reverse side of the hill,
        you feel,
sits Satan, ready for a meal;

to have and be the entrée there
might be your destiny in Hell.
        The smell
of intercourse and pubic hair
        (God's toast),
the sin against the Holy Ghost,

burn in your brains like autumn leaves,
you reckon the venereal trap,
        like clap,
is sprung by this. Each one believes
        girls rammed,
badgered or rabbited, are damned.

You two have Envy as your friend.
Fear and Unkindness know you well,
        the bell
rings often at Enjoyment's End,
        where tea
is served to Pride, Unholy Glee;

Gossip and Bossiness, bosom pals,
are free to sit and to admire
        the fire,
can stretch their legs and smoke Pall Malls.
        Miss Hate
will stay particularly late.

Egged on by them, self-satisfied,
you tell us what we may not do,
        the coo
of pigeons is a switchback ride
        to Sin –
and the seductive violin.

Propriety in public! Write
only what nurseries think and need –
        your creed
is always this – and not what might
        (no!) stir
sex-feeling in a him or her.

And these are your instructions we
at our own risk refuse, deny!
        You sigh
that so much wickedness could be
        in life!
The standard husband, standard wife,

are all that are permitted in
your limited philosophy,
        the knee
is very naughty; whisky, gin
        are bad.
Thinking of such things makes you sad.

Without *you* to work out their will,
Pride, Envy, Hate and all that crew,
        Fear too,
could not force-feed their bitter pill.
        It's sweet
when 'Morals' make it fit to eat.

This is your function in our land,
you are the servants of a No,
        all so
prudent and pudent, underhand –
        I doubt
if we will ever throw you out!

46

On First Looking into Michael Grant's Cities of Vesuvius

In battledress, yes, I was there. That dramatic great
                                    wartime eruption
          spewed out the red-hot shit; it looked very splendid
                                    at night
crushing the villas and trees, and the ash came down, a
                                    red-purple,
          to the depth of an old-fashioned foot. We moved the
                                    trucks and the guns
for safety. But our letters home were security-minded.
                                    No mention.
          You needed a four-wheel drive to churn through
                                    that stuff on the road.
This was in March '44 (as the clubland talks would
                                    remind you),
          of Europe's one active volcano the last recorded
                                    display.

Before this happened, I took, on an outing, a party of
                                    gunners
          (we weren't operational then) to Pompeii; they
                                    wanted the church,
the wine-shops, the cheap souvenirs. I opted, alone, for
                                    the *Scavi*.
          I had one guide to myself – and paid with a tin of
                                    corned beef.
We covered a lot of the ground. His English was good
                                    but not perfect –
          I was pleased to hear of a king whose name seemed
                                    to be Charles the Turd.
Although I went there three times – with a friend on
                                    two visits –
          and the guide remarked with a grin, as we looked at
                                    the rough plaster thighs,

47

how it was obvious enough that the body we saw was a
                                                woman.
        We went round the brothel as well. He lit up the
                                        paintings on walls
with a candle held high; you could see where each girl's
                                        speciality, pictured
above the door of her room, enticed you inside to
                                                her skill.
He unlocked for us, too, with his key, that famous and
                                        frivolous fresco
        which shows the soldier who weighs his huge
                                uncircumcised cock
on the scales, and the gold goes up – for pleasure's more
                                        precious than money.
        Behind us, by accident, there (for this is inside a
                                        house door)
an American nurse walked by. She gave a great 'Oo!' and
                                                fled, shaken.
        I don't know what it's like now. But *Off Limits*
                                        would, then, be the words;
and the delicate souls of the girls were protected, the
                                        brothel was banned; though
plain enough in the road you could see a large
                                        bas-relief tool
to point the vernacular way to the house dedicated to
                                                Venus.
        With a naked foot, on dark nights, it must have been
                                        useful, at that.
Herculaneum wasn't so good. The best thing of all was
                                                the statue
        that shows Pan at work on a goat. This was our
                                        verdict, at least.

So, Grant, you swim into my ken. With your writing, so
                                        large and clear, telling
of thirty-three years ago now – more or less, give or
                                        take, to the day
when the boil on the neck of the land burst, on the
                                        warlike eighteenth
and we stood with our drinks, there, to watch, on
                                the roof of the officers' mess,

how the lava rolled down in the dark, a slow raw mass on
the skyline.
We didn't think so much, then, of the suffering; how
those who died
choked in the chemical fumes – like the brave and
inquisitive Pliny,
like the dog at the end of its chain. That's one of the
things about war.
The dying was commonplace, then. It was interesting,
more than distressing.
And of course you're entirely right, the gladiatorial
shows
were disgusting (as Seneca said); more so than the
drinking and fucking.
Dr Arnold, the father, who wrote that the Bay of
Naples was one
long drama (and 'fearsome' too) of Sin and Death, and,
yes, Pleasure,
got it wrong in his Puritan way – and so did his
talented son.
Why should there be shame? No one lived (as you say) to
be much over forty –
over most of the world, to this day, that's an average
life.

We are exceptions, aloof and well-dressed in our
self-conscious cities.
If any small British town, perhaps a resort like
Torquay,
were quickly hermetically sealed, volcanoed and covered
for ever,
would archaeologists find such a high standard of
art?
Architecture, as well. I think you make a good point
there.
I know they crucified slaves. There was cruelty, but
easiness too;
the easiness of a land where the passions could be quite
volcanic
but with the blue sea and sky there was always
benevolent sun.

49

The Doll Made by my Dead Sister

A doll 33 cm high
made throughout of felt –
I prop her up in front of me as I write –
dressed in Victorian clothes
(pieces of women's dresses)
with a full skirt reaching to the ground.

But this doll is a lie –
and that mouth where butter wouldn't melt –
turn her inside out, she's as black as night,
as black as sloes,
confounding all guesses,
turned upside down, skirt over head . . . There, aproned
    and gowned,

stands a plantation slave
and under her ballooning skirt
is the head of the other (red wool hair, green eyes),
invisible; so each
is an opposite in a way . . .
though neither has legs, neither has private parts –

amateur psychiatrists would rave
and knowingly dish the dirt,
saying 'Escape from sex!' with excited cries,
two girls with no breech . . .
that's what they used to say,
but there's more to it than that, even in these simple crafts
    and arts.

The Moment

There are even photographs of it:
the moment when, for the first time,
in that tense, expectant landscape,
the enemy troops appear.

There they are, advancing –
Germans from World War One
running with rifles.
As, from far back in time, so many others.

You are the opposing infantry –
this means you.
Your brain falters. *This
is it*, you think,

*these are the ones we've heard
so much about.* Like old people
when, for the first time, they confront
the unambiguous symptoms.

The Doggerel of Life

Yeats, who admired Robert Bridges
and his poems about linnets,
who wouldn't have lasted five minutes
at their Menin Gates and Vimy Ridges,
cut out from his great Ox Book
the Owens and Rosenbergs. But look,

Dorothy Wellesley is there, crazy,
and Flecker, whom iambics tempted like houris;
nothing could be more vacuous than Rabindranath
    Tagore is;
or, than W.J. Turner, more romantic and hazy;
or more of an ugly rhyming zombie
than that great genius Lascelles Abercrombie.

So what he missed was the vivid actual factual.
In a way he emerged from his youthful Celtic Twilight,
gazing at the moon through a Dublin skylight,
but he was very selective, describing what was tactual –
the copulation of the nymph and gland-boosted satyr.
The hot blood of a machine-gunned friend was a very
    different matter.

Kipling's Imperialism and Ours

(The Light That Failed)

If you call a spade a spade,
those wars were really trade
and the box-wallahs had it made.

As trade follows the flag
the guy with the carpet-bag
brings dollars and jet-lag.

Right Wing strong-arm regimes
help the market, it seems,
in those Latin American dreams.

Red satellites gather round
like sheep in a pound
and applause is the only sound.

The massacres, black by white,
are an artistic sight
in the African day or night.

In Kipling's Sudan, war dead
made patterns of colour, he said,
decomposed composition, and led

his artist-hero to rave
of the multichrome deaths of the brave,
while the Queen they were out to save

sat there and loved John Brown
as he drank the whisky down
and the beauties went on the town.

The Animals in the Adelaide Zoo

The animals in the Adelaide Zoo are very comfortable.
It's a small zoo but very well organized.
The elephant stands in a small space but seems happy.
The black-backed jackals run; hunting, hunting,
    hunting.
A slow loris moves quiet in nocturnal lighting.
The black panther is a melanistic form of the spotted
    leopard.

The animals in the Adelaide Zoo are not rhetorical.
The zebras are not torn apart by lions.
The hippopotamus is in happy water.
The giraffe's sex organs are as high as your head.
The jaguars and ocelots attack nothing.
Everything is as it should be in the Adelaide Zoo.

The animals in the Adelaide Zoo are already in Heaven.
Their children are born lucky, nobody hates them.
They are surrounded by love and regular food.
Their lives are without drama, they show no fear.
Eviscerated on a path lies a tiny indigenous mouse.
In their cages, they show no concern, in the Adelaide
    Zoo.

Ode on the Death of the Air Commodore

For E.J. Thribb

Oh, Commodore!
You will never drink anything any more!
No more beer, gin, brandy, whisky or wine
that made you feel so fine
and roll down the street lurching out of bars
and causing consternation among cars!

Oh, Commodore!
You have flown to God on that further shore!
You lived in gin with Lady Blank,
drinking like two fishes in a fish tank –
this made your brain soften and your arteries harden
and when she locked you out you slept in the garden!

Oh, Commodore!
Alcohol is a deceiver and a most conspicuous whore!
Perhaps I should mention
that every week you drew an Air Commodore's pension
and poured it into the glasses in local pubs,
an old bad-tempered lion and far from its cubs!

Oh, Commodore!
That once-goodlooking head must often have been sore!
You might easily have choked on your own vomit
but, as it happened, far from it –
far quicker and cleaner, a heart attack
as you lay there, completely pissed, on your back!

Oh, Commodore!
Were you once a pilot in Korea, or in the Second World
    War?
Did you fly bombers or fighters, incredibly brave,
before something gave
and to this one drug you became such a terrible slave?
What went wrong? The Devil is very possessive –
he blotted you out, asphasiac and aggressive!

Oh, Commodore!
Believers say there is Mercy, God doesn't shut the door.
You often had to be helped home,
and all roads lead to Death, as they once did to Rome,
and indeed your life can't have been very funny –
far too much drinking, too much spare time and money!

The Lovesleep

In an exciting world of love-bites, nipple-nipping,
unbuttoning and unzipping,
kisses that are
the highest kind of communication,
the lovers experience their timeless elation;

perhaps they reach those peaks where, like a bomb
    exploding,
the angels sing, encoding
ecstasies that
our language can never really deal with –
its nouns and its adjectives that no one can feel with;

but when the woman lies in the man's arms – soft,
    sleeping,
in perfect trust and keeping
faith, you might say,
that is the truest peace and disarming –
no one can sleep in the arms of an enemy, however
    charming.

Rape of the Fly

These sausages are blood-bespattered pigs,
these eggs from jungle fowl. These naked chickens
are hornbills only fit for making soup.
The critics are the natives, words like stones,
that make derisive gestures but don't kill,
canoes all round, but I pursue my course.
The lovely ladies, birds of paradise,
flirting the tops of highest mountain trees!
Like the uncritical women of the tribes
they lie there, opening admiring legs.
The weighty letters to the *Herald*
are monstrous droppings of the cassowary.

The speeches and the books, the late Awards –
the rivalry, who's best and who's next best –
the Medals for the sailing through the swamp.
Our sex-mad novelists, gigantic genitals,
hopping aboard with elephantiasis!
Grossly inflated reputations! Only we
whose dysentery, malaria, beri-beri
proclaim us obstinate and purposeful,
deserve this world, so like the one we left.

Still in my dreams I visit that great Island,
I mapped it and I know it, mile by mile.

I miss the mosquitoes and the arrowheads,
the shrivelled corpses wrapped in bark, the skulls
trophying a longhouse – 150 yards –
navigating the tireless looping sandbanked river,
pushing upstream against the current's flow
with engine power that scarcely made us move.

This was my one achievement, my reward
a country where the missionaries are savage.

NOTE *Rape Of The Fly* is an account of the exploration
of New Guinea in the 1870s, written by John Goode. The
Fly is the main river. The poem is supposed to be a
reminiscence by Lawrence Hargrave, the engineer, who
later fell out with D'Albertis, the leader of the Expedi-
tion. He makes a comparison with the 'civilization'
of Sydney.

The Little Girl Writes a Sonnet about her Dead Cat

I do not hope to see my cat again
or look upon that friendly furry face
in some imagined, altered, other place
where there is never ice or hail or rain
or bitter wind or cutting of the sleet
or falling, drifting, animal-hating snow
that slants down drearily, both fast and slow,
to gem his coat or wet his feline feet.

That there's Cat Heaven, kitten-having-fun,
I don't believe – where any cat can lie
stretched out like streaky bacon, always fed,
happy and purring in perpetual sun.
I'm sorry for my cat, he had to die –
but I still love him, even though he's dead.

Tears are Round, the Sea is Deep: Roll them Overboard and Sleep

Though I am old and dirty
it wasn't always so
my face looked very different
forty years ago

I know you can't own people
though the law thinks you can
a man is a man is a man is a man
but not a married man

They can't be forced to like you
by anything you do
you can't make love by willpower
and women know this too

It's only by behaving
with no thought for effect
that we become attractive
escaping that neglect

which hugs the constant lover
the worshipper of tears
who attracts nothing to himself
except the fate he fears

I don't say be indifferent
just don't expect defeat
or else that tragic programme
will head for a repeat

To think one's lovable or nice
is always very hard
this is the province of the cad
and the fast-talking card

But still a man is something
you can't deny he's there
don't put him down or sit on him
he isn't like a chair

for folding up to put away
in garden shed or loft
and women too are human beings
and more than sweet and soft

they have their thoughts and feelings
behind their bobbling fronts
it isn't all beauty beauty
and sex and silly cunts

So though I'm old and dirty
and funny in the head
I think I've learned a thing or two
before I drop down dead.

O Yongë Fresshë Folkës, Hee or Shee

They look so beautiful, that's how they look –
but none of them has been into a book.
They look so fresh and innocent (because they've got to)
however hard they try (they do try) not to.
Yet evil's there, unseen or just subliminal,
a baby face can be that of a criminal.

While we look full of woe, and vice untold,
simply because we happen to be old.
Tired eyes, a stoop, a neck so like a vulture's –
these are the hallmarks of our silver Cultures.
They have the Force, testiculate or clitorate,
we – for our pains – the joy of being literate!

The Owls are Leaving

The owls are leaving town, in a strong procession.
They stream into the side streets, to the squares,
They fill the squares and block the avenues.
They move in silence. They are eight feet tall.

The owls are leaving town, with a sure precision.
Their eyes look straight ahead, they do not turn,
Their features clothe them in a secret wisdom.
No looking back. Each one is three feet broad.

The owls are leaving town, with no hint of passion.
They shuffle forwards, they are calm and good,
Their feet expect the texture of the roadway.
They never loved us. They are birds that go.

The Deaths

On the plains the lions walk among the herds of
wildebeeste like policemen or soldiers among the
citizens, not using their power, peaceful and not
destructive. Occasionally they run them, get them
going. Perhaps they don't kill, but in the galloping herd
the running tires a weak one. Next time round, he is
singled out, isolated and caught. The catcher throttles –
then the tearing. The pride lopes up, it's a family picnic.
Hyenas, vultures, tidy all the scraps.

Surely our deaths are like this, surely the deaths walk
round with us; at home, on city streets? Not showing
their claws, since they need only wait, they trot beside us
like obedient dogs. The old, the tired, the ill are run to a
fall – a date is at their throats, the deathday date. They
wear it like a collar. They too are dogs.

Self-knowledge

Why does it always come as a surprise
to realise there are people who dislike you,
when an uncomplimentary word (like *shit* or *bitch*)
is reported as used to describe you?
They are fierce against you as hawks, undovable –
and you always imagined you were so lovable!

Of course they may have got you wrong;
or they may hate you simply because you're English
or French or American; there are many stereotypes.
Instant hatred is very easy.
Class can bring it on, perhaps, your way of speaking –
what *you* think's refined *they* consider a twitlike
    squeaking.

But remember, even murderers don't think they're
  wicked.
Hitler, for example, thought he was helping Germany
by killing all those horrible Jews and subversive Reds.
He never regarded *himself* as ghastly.
So that might comfort you. *Let there be light!* Be
glad to learn you're not as nice as you might be!

Pian dei Giullari

Never go back, they say. Never go back.
I went back.

With my twenty-one-year-old daughter
I walked through the Porta Romana,
up the Erta Canina,
round the curved Giramonte
and high beyond the city.

I was twice as old as then.
A lot of it I didn't recognize,
I thought we were lost –
till a name startled me into recognition:
Pian dei Giullari.
A small hilly road
but there, as in sentimental dreams,
was the straight drive through the olive orchard,
the house in faded orange with barred windows,
our once Headquarters.

And there, almost opposite,
the entrance to her villa
where 28 embraced 16.

Was this sad or happy?

Our weak, nice Major died
(I saw his obituary by accident),
the love affair came to nothing.

In those days we were careless —
as the war was careless of us.
Nobody thought very far ahead.
Girls were like wine for the drinking.

The landscape that we saw from our windows
in a time of cicadas and nightingales
stood there unaltered.
I looked at it and felt the warm lightness
of khaki drill on my shoulders.

Montale

As I stood among the wild lettuce
in that desolate sexlandscape
with the autumnal green of late August,
I thought of Montale,
of the bits and pieces of the past
that keep us hermetic.

Somewhere there was a river,
a tidal river
sluggish with low water.
With its help, I knew,
woodbits and old bottles
had climbed the concrete bank.
It was all mud and concrete
but I couldn't see it.
It had, even, its complement of sailors.
It handed out driftwood.

But I stood alone in wild lettuce,
a plant that doesn't exist,
clumping the rough fairway
to an overgrown golf course,
distant neutral buildings
and the figures of cricketers,
open land — and its name was Sadness.

There were paths, but vague ones,
I could have stayed, I could have
gone in any direction.
I went to the river.

A Punk Turkish March for Christopher on his Giving Paintings by my Dead Sister to my Children

(terkib-i bend)★

Not since the reign of Bayezit the Thunderbolt
and the days when the Beloved was moon-faced,
almond-eyed, eyebrows two bows, eyelashes arrows,
has a poet been given such a pleasing emotional jolt,
a kind of mental orgasm (let's not be strait-laced)
in a life whose perspective inevitably narrows!

I'm overjoyed to hear what you did –
giving one of *her* pictures to each kid.

So much feeling attaches to an artefact
(all art is imperfect, this doggerel most
of all perhaps – you can't rival God,
said the Moslems, who botched every creative act),
good or bad, her painting haunts us like a ghost
and means more than Be-Bop, Rock, Reggae or Mod.

This is because we all understand
each brush-stroke was made by a once-living hand.

★ 'Metrical lines could also be grouped into stanzas, or *bend*, of from
four to ten lines, though the longer groupings are very rare. The *terc-i
bend*, where the stanzas are separated by a repeated rhyming couplet,
and the *terkib-i bend*, where the rhyming couplet changes each time,
are forms used for philosophic or contemplative poems.'
– Nermin Menemencioğlu: *The Penguin Book of Turkish Verse*

We see her physically there, in front of the easel,
each canvas is a presence as real as her face,
more charged than the instant smiling photograph
(like a happy rabbit unaware of the weasel)
and proves she didn't vanish without trace,
though Time, in our philosophy, has the last laugh.

And even Shakespeare, one day, will be gone.
The clocks like policemen are crying *Move on!*

We can't remember her as a statue on a plinth
or frozen in the fixed epithets of the old *divan* poet –
though you *could* say that once her cheeks were rose
and her hair *could* be described as hyacinth,
her teeth as pearls (court verse, wouldn't you know it!).
The things we remember her by are not these.

The visual images blur and grow faint –
but her pictures are still there, as fresh as paint.

The Dying Animals

The animals that look at us like children
in innocence, in perfect innocence!
The innocence that looks at us! Like children
the animals, the simple animals,
have no idea why legs no longer work.

The food that is refused, the love of sleeping –
in innocence, in childhood innocence
there is a parallel of love. Of sleeping
they're never tired, the dying animals;
sick children too, whose play to them is work.

The animals are little children dying,
brash tigers, household pets – all innocence,
the flames that lit their eyes are also dying,
the animals, the simple animals,
die easily; but hard for us, like work!

'And Female Smells in Shuttered Rooms'

Short square fingers stuffing pipes
and Kilpeck witches in the streets,
all the Apeneck Sweeney types
riding women, staining sheets!

Sensitives wince into the world,
it seems to them so rough and coarse;
French poets, filigreed and pearled,
are better than a wingèd horse

and perfumes floating round an arm
than the crude odours of the groin –
foul Circe with her porcine charm
and Charon with his deadly coin!

★   ★   ★

Once, Eliot, I was shy as you
and impotent as you (I guess);
I failed at what I tried to do,
my sex-life was an awful mess.

But Stephen, Wystan, Christopher
enjoyed themselves with loads of boys,
they did not hesitate, demur,
or shrink from treating them like toys.

The lad is sad who masturbates.
It's good but not quite good enough –
though (once) was good enough for Yeats.
The wet warmth of that furry muff,

the girlish kiss, attracted still,
tiptilted tits, the big-eyed gaze –
I ended feeling rather ill;
I missed my homosexual phase.

A forest, round about, of cocks
grew up, a sexual Sacred Wood,
to flaunt Eternity, mock clocks;
and there, alone, I weeping stood.

Those others kicked the gong around –
Tom, Dick (especially Dick) and Harry
gave them the bliss I never found.
They even took time off to marry.

A nightmare (you could call it) and
the worse because I was so young –
Love seemed a Never Never Land.
Like Keats, infected in the lung,

I yearned for Light that never was
(there's not much fun in lonely yearning)
and this was made much worse because
I wasn't in a job and earning.

So unemployed and unenjoyed,
I sipped my bitter, loveless cup –
until, like Fathers out of Freud,
the bloody Army took me up!

Homeric Hymn

When Apollo's about
a brightness is all around,
it shines and shines on the ground,
a comet that stares you out,

you know a remarkable god
is helping to bend your mind
and you will unerringly find
it isn't a con or a cod

but a genuine daylight ghost,
an undeniable fact,
telling you how to act –
and more demanding than most.

He'll grant the half of the prayer,
but it will be only the half,
not the cow but the calf –
you mustn't ask more than your share,

nothing is quite all right
and nothing goes all your way,
Apollo may rule the day
but he can't put a stop to night,

granting a prayer entire
is something gods seldom do,
the ones that are happy are few
and you risk the Olympian fire

if you protest too much
or boast in your human pride –
the roughness of the ride
is surely reserved for such;

so make it a modest plea
for fame or fortune or love –
Venus might come, with a dove
or two, from the sexy sea –

and say to yourself 'That's fine!'
when blessings come in disguise.
The gods, with ironical eyes,
are devious, but divine.

The Crumbs of Sex and Comfort

The crumbs of sex and comfort
that fall an old man's way
are for a rainy day,
demand judicious hoarding –
they're few and far between
but valuable, I mean,

and love is rare, and rarer
as energy grows faint.
The patience of a saint
is needed in a lifetime
of waiting for the joy
that every girl and boy

is taught is round the corner.
Romance! deluding word!
imaginary bird
that flies out iridescent
in adolescent dreams!
Soft flesh (like chocolate creams)

although we grow maturer
won't quite lose its appeal
(the two ways that we feel),
the taste, perhaps, of childhood
but in our late decades
never entirely fades

and vanishes for ever –
there still is nothing much
the ecstasy of touch
won't better in the moment
of the triumphant cry
that love is honoured by.

Women Over 40 Are Perfect

The respectable ladies who think it's so
disgusting
that teenage girls should sink so low
as lusting
for the goodlooking companionable boys
have not been, in their time, averse to such joys;

many of these saints have had one (or two)
abortions –
nobody speaks of them (well, would *you*?),
distortions
of an instinct, the kind of mistakes
that an innocent girl very often makes,

hushed-up, of course, it's understood,
and private,
in the best conditions money could
contrive it,
victims of the rich alcoholic sperm.
But these young ones must go to the full term,

because they've surely got to be taught
a lesson,
sluts that they are, and *caught* –
you'd guess an
unholy public nuisance had come to light
from the pure drivel that those moral madams write.

PART TWO
The So-Called Sonnets

Sonnet: Danish Blue

From Copenhagen reports come in
of an American film marked 'Genuine Porn';
it all takes place in a hospital (a favourite scene)
where pretty nurses with glasses fellate male patients
(artificial masturbation?) and there's some joker
who keeps putting Spanish Fly into the drinking water
so that meetings of the Management Committee end up
    as orgies
and the woman President (with all the other girls) loses
    her knickers.

In particular, and this film is called *Sweet Freedom*,
the Doctor with the very biggest organ
is ramming it (in the interests of Science – orgone
    research)
into a really permissive dark-haired naked beauty.
As he does so she cries (male fantasy): 'Oh, fuck it, fuck
    it, fuck it!'
A real woman, as anybody knows, would cry: 'Fuck *me*!'

Sonnet: The Greedy Man Considers Nuclear War

I suppose you all realize we shall lose the sizzling sausages
and the mild mountains of mashed potatoes!
Boiled silverside with dumplings, raspberries and cream!
We shall vanish from the pecking order of the tikka
    chicken,

trout with almonds will swim away from us,
little lambs no more will jump into our mouths,
fragrant with rosemary; all the good wholesome food
will vanish just as surely as sophisticated dishes!

And what shall we be left with? Some assorted politicians
not very good to eat, some dispirited root crops,
tinned food perhaps – everything else burned up,
the culture of the kitchen, the chef's wisdom of the ages
vanished in a flame like the bread in a toaster!
The end of eating civilization as we know it!

Sonnet: The Red Fairy Book

I remember as a child I used to be terrified
by the illustrations to those stories that Andrew Lang
    collected,
where Princes were likely to be chopped into little pieces,
something nasty lived in the lake, and nine-headed Trolls
were decapitated by some good-hearted simpleton.
There was also a horrible Japanese animal
that spoke when it was cut into joints that hung from the
    ceiling
and because of its pleading was finally reconstituted and
    dangerous. . . .

But in fact the real world, now that I know it,
turns out to be quite a good deal more horrible –
where men are skinned alive and castrated,
where various emblems are stuck into women,
there's self-righteous torture (electric chairs and
    hanging).
And nothing can be remedied, as in fairy stories.

Sonnet: The Hymn-Singers

We're officer cadets in 1940 –
and some of us won't get out of this war alive.
There's snow, and ice, on the gun park. With freezing
   hands
we bring the gun into action (so many seconds flat).
Later, in pubs, we sing the rugger songs,
establishing the warmth of wartime camaraderie,
like women's sewing bees, one sex together,
making a joke of love we're frightened of. . . .

Years later will come the impotent polymaths
to say we shouldn't have sung them. Though very young
   men
think women and battle are equally tests, they'll say
it's homosexual. But we were a Congregation,
hymn-singing in that darkness – so would you!
Those sex-linked Spartans knew a thing or two!

Sonnet: The Light and the Dark

You say: Why are all the poems about the dark side of
   marriage?
About the rows, the screaming, the differences of
   opinion.
I say (because I like arguing?) that very few of them are –
but in any case poems are general and not to be
   interpreted literally
and they're also a kind of cure for the bad parts of life.
Stating a problem is itself, in a way, a solution.
Happiness is the one emotion a poem can't capture,
there are very few sonnets that purr with contentment.

But here goes! To be in a warm bed with somebody
   friendly,
to be looked after, cooked for, cared for; these are not
   nothings.

Conversation and fun, companionship, Twenty
    Questions,
humming the Verdi, Puccini, Bellini. . . .
Do I have to write it out in words: *I love you*,
after the fondness of a quarter of a century?

Sonnet: Comics

The comics know their way about (they always have),
they know they can raise the giggling laugh by saying
'He has very heavy commitments', 'He's got a large
    overdraft'
or 'Take down her particulars!' It's standard,
oblique references to cocks, balls, breasts, even (by way
    of pussies)
cunts. And this is how the Puritans like it,
it's exactly like scratching something that itches
(hence prurience); it's sly and not direct. Though
    pleasurable.

But if you use the words, describe the actions, they go up
    in flames.
Somehow they are not easy (we are not easy)
about being sexual creatures. They won't accept
that at best we're thinking animals. So keep it dark.
The preachers and the comics are in league.
Creating and dispersing thoughts of guilt.

Sonnet: Cat Death

But how, they seriously say, can you ever compare
the death of your mother to the death of your cat?
I answer: easily. After she had the pin in her hip-joint,
as she haltingly pushed her walking-frame towards the
    loo
she simply foreshadowed his slow limping progress,
with the bone-cancer distorting his harmed right
    shoulder,
towards the cat-pan, the cat-tray (whetever you call it).
Both of these, to see, were equally pathetic.

And as she lay in the hospital, with noisy breathing,
hardly eating, seldom conscious; and as *he* lay,
in unhappy lethargy, not touching his food,
drinking a little, liquid intake only – surely he deserved
equally the drug that pushed him into unconsciousness
and it was good that both were separated from pain?

PART THREE

Dreams

So I have this recurring dream. My publisher tells me that a new Editor has been put in charge of me and all my works; and I go along to the publisher's office and there, lo and behold! the Editor turns out to be an Editress, and she is sitting there ready to discuss my new book of poems – which lies in typescript before her.

She is a neat, tidy, well-turned-out lady of fifty or so, with gaudily rimmed spectacles and an owl-like look, blue rinse hair. She explains that the Poetry Readers' Association, of which she is President, will not like a lot of the poems in this book (which she has photostatted and circulated to all her membership). She quotes a letter received from a housewife in Esher, which says: 'This book is sheer filth. I tremble to think what would happen if it were left lying about the house for young children to read!' A domesticated Professor has written: 'This kind of pornography is anti-life.'

The Editress picks up a big blue pencil, about a foot long, and begins – with the utmost savagery – to score great diagonal lines through the poems not approved of. In the end one poem only is left, its innocence established. This is about feeding a horse with lumps of sugar. I leave the office feeling I am lucky not to be arrested.

The other form of the dream (for this is a serial dream and exists in two parts) is exactly as above except that the Editor turns out to be a very serious smartly dressed American. He is called Chuck. 'Glad to meet up with you!' and 'I'm mighty pleased to have the opportunity to talk with you!' he says, and 'Hopefully, now, we can get some place!'

His view is that all the poems should be rewritten by him and then re-presented to me for a joint consultation. He starts to go through them: 'The end of this one ought to be at the beginning!' he says, and (when he comes to the word 'expedient') 'The kids'll never understand this!' He explains to me that in Iowa nobody has ever heard of Telemann or Ronald Firbank – nor has he ('Who they?' he asks). He criticizes the poems for lack of positive thinking. 'These are all *negative* poems, Gavin!' (we have been on first name terms since the first moment of meeting). In the end no poems are left unscathed; they are all bowdlerized, simplified, run through the cliché-machine. No one line is more than two words long.

As in the first dream, I wake drowned in sweat, with a feeling of criminal inadequacy.

Elegiac Verses for a Dead Headmaster

'I would prefer' was your name (if you translated it out of
                                    the Latin),
        appropriate in every way, a Classical Scholar like
                                    you
should have been very well pleased. You enunciated so
                                    clearly
        no syllable ever escaped, blurred, unincisive or
                                    vague,
'the circle' (you said) 'of the teeth'. From Homer, the
                        ἕρκος 'οδόντων.
        You had a robinlike stance as you stood there
                        before the whole school

telling us, humorous, firm, about the Speech Day
                                    arrangements –
        'two tents with the singular appellations: Tent A
                                    and Tent B',
confident, twitched your black gown; our laughter was
                                cautious and servile,
        for halolike over your head your Power hung – to
                                beat and expel.
When the strong rulers relax, it could be a very good
                                    omen
        but nobody likes to take risks. We giggled a bit at
                                the hymn
we sang in the Chapel, that said 'in constancy follow the
                                    Master'.
        You were a poet, though, too – at Marlborough
                                write a School Song,
'The Wind That Blows Over The Downs', and, later,
                                light verse was your forte.
        In Canada you write a piece that comically
                                mentioned Moose Jaw
and equally Medicine Hat; a Conference, this, of
                                    Headmasters?
        (that seems the fittingest term, as lions have their
                                pride and the geese
their gaggle and virgins occur in a giggle when nouns are
                                    collective).
        You read this aloud to the school, an 'ego trip'
                                someone might say,
but after all, where is the harm? There certainly were
                                some Headmasters
        whose views were unpleasantly pi – you were
                                more liberal than that.
'I don't like' you once said (not to me) 'this young man
                                D.H. Lawrence!'
        two years after his death; we smiled at this
                                Philistine view.
His *Letters* I had as a prize I didn't ask you to sign – you
        probably wouldn't approve. Your wife to a
                                musical friend

explained how you never should shut, not ever, the top
of a piano.
If you shut it, she cried, damp air is shut in with
the keys!
At some educational moot you sat (so he said) next to
Auden –
he was surprised you were such a peaceful,
scholarly man,
not major-generally or given to military bluster,
as one could surely expect, knowing the name of
the school.

You lived to be terribly old and when you died you were
ninety,
forgetting the names of the boys and even the
names of the staff.
You frightened me when I was young, but I was a
nervous young shaver.
In the Elysian fields this is a form you will know
(you told me once that my name, grammatically, ought
to be Thouart).
It isn't Latin or Greek; but a tribute, nevertheless.

Jubilate Matteo

For I rejoice in my cat Matty.
For his coat is variegated in black and brown, with white
undersides.
For in every way his whiskers are marvellous.
For he resists the Devil and is completely neuter.
For he sleeps and washes himself and walks warily in the
ways of Putney.
For he is at home in the whole district of SW15.
For in this district the great Yorkshire Murderer ate his
last meal before he entered into captivity.
For in the Book of Crime there is no name like John
Reginald Halliday Christie.
For Yorkshire indeed excels in all things, as Geoffrey
Boycott is the best Batsman.

80

For the Yorkshire Ripper and the Hull Arsonist have their horns exalted in glory.

For Yorkshire is therefore acknowledged the greatest County.

For Hull was once of the company, that is now of Humberside.

For Sir Leonard Hutton once scored 364 runs in a Test Match.

For Fred Trueman too is a flagrant glory to Yorkshire.

For my cat wanders in the ways of the angels of Yorkshire.

For in his soul God has shown him a remarkable vision of Putney.

For he has also trodden in the paths of the newly fashionable.

For those who live in Gwendolen Avenue cry 'Drop dead, darling!'

For in Cambalt Road and Dealtry Road where the Vet lives there are professional people.

For Erpingham Road and Danemere Street and Dryburgh Road include the intelligentsia.

For in Clarendon Drive the British Broadcasting Corporation is rampant.

For the glory of God has deserted the simple.

For the old who gossiped in Bangalore Road are unknown to the dayspring.

For there is a shortage of the old people who adorned the novels of William Trevor.

For in the knowledge of this I cling to the old folkways of Gwalior Road and Olivette Street.

For I rejoice in my cat, who has the true spirit of Putney.

Double Dactyl: Emily Dickinson *

Stay-At-Home-Fey-At-Home
Emily Dickinson
Wrote – in a Kind of Un-
dotty – Clipt – Morse –

Capital Letters – God –
Lucifugosity –
Dashes – a Cart before
Such a Dark Horse!

* This poem was a winner of a *New Statesman* Competition.

An Old Larkinian

When I think of the crumby poetry
    people turn out to honour some pseuds
and Old Pretenders (and you must know it!) – *re*
    Art, alas, there are always such feuds –
so many whom Kingsley would simply call shags
or, if female, could be regarded as hags
    or old bags,

are enshrined in collectors' items, *Festschriften*,
    that others think give verse a bad name.
So it's like taking sides, saying 'I was at Clifton'
    or 'I'm an Etonian', no one can blame
poets for being admirers well-versed in one another
like a worshipping schoolboy younger brother
    or a mother

proud of the son's or daughter's achievements,
    sticking the pins of the journey into the map,
following them through loves and bereavements,
    seeing them off each morning in a school cap,
more than terribly pleased when they make the team,
celebrating the Knighthood with a joyful scream;
    a sunbeam

indeed he seems, or she! I'm a Larkinian
    and glad to acknowledge it to all;
though I know that death has a lot of dominion
    my admiration for your verse is not small,
you are far the best of the lonely scullers
and I'm proud to wear, among solemners and dullers,
    your colours.

Preserved

In the blurbs of the old slim volumes
they used to write:
'These are all the poems that Mr Stringfellow
wishes to preserve.'

At once there is an image of flat
copper preserving pans bubbling away
in a big kitchen, and of Mr Stringfellow
pouring, stirring, sealing the Kilner jars.

In fact there may be as much difference
between real living experience and his verse
as there is between the fresh beautiful raspberries
and the artificiality of jam.

Mackintosh Madrigal

My purple face, my yellow teeth,
    My little tiny eyes,
My snuffling and my nightly snores,
Unpleasing even to the whores,
    No longer prompt a young girl's sighs
    As she lies soft beneath, ho ho!
    As she lies soft beneath!
    Ho ho!

My pursed-up mouth, my aching back,
  My memory half gone,
My eyes walked over by the crows,
Unfashionable, ill-fitting clothes,
    Will never bring a Great Love on –
    Me in my dirty mac, ho ho!
    Me in my dirty mac!
    Ho ho!

The Lively Arts?

Bohemian Life goes on, the same as ever, untiringly.
'She threw a full bottle of wine at the wall!' they say,
  admiringly.
At the parties they all behave violently or insultingly.
'He poured his whisky all over her!' they say, exultingly.
'I love passionate people like that!' they say, adoringly.
But it follows a pattern (besides the waste of alcohol)
  really quite boringly.

In a bar with muzak once, I was told (unless I'm
  dreaming)
a neurotic wife said 'If you don't turn that music off, I
  shall start screaming!'
and they didn't – and she did; it was high-pitched, very
  effective.
To deduce the chaos this caused, you don't need to be a
  detective.
But those parties! A critic in a corner is bringing his lunch
  up
and two poets are getting ready for a first-class
  punch-up.

In the fifties once, a man introduced somebody as Dylan
  Thomas
(a pure mistake, in all good faith) and, without dotting i's
  or putting in commas,
this fellow clocked him – knocked him flat as a kipper.

He thought he was taking the mickey. So begin to hunt
    for your glass slipper
and slip away before midnight, is my advice to the
    literate.
Avant-garde behaviour (when it's pissed) is never very
    considerate.

The Victorian Husband
(Before the Murder)

Each morning, coffee cold as ice,
His thoughts to one thought carried:
How nice to be happily married,
To be married to somebody nice!

With mangled muffins and bad tea,
As insults were being parried,
He thought: To be happily married,
To be married to someone like me!

If I were rich – that would suffice!
I should not be so harried.
I should be happily married
To somebody really nice!

A Little Traditional Song: Of Love

They say women don't go for
pure sex
as men go for it.
Men are less fussy –
put their arms round the necks
of the housewife *and* the hussy.

They say women don't welcome
bed games
like men, don't welcome
that Pink Intruder –
like to know lovers' names,
only loved ones can get ruder.

They say women love people
not parts.
The love's for him, *him*,
(touch goes with emotion),
not for his loving arts,
lips and hands like soothing lotion.

They say women, etc.
They say!
No, no, not always!
Films, books, get bluer,
there's the Pill, day by day
all such women are fewer!

Hear the Voice of the Bard!

The Poet likes to float down from the sky,
complete and comfortable from on high –
    he knows he's in a state of Grace,
    making his Kingsley Amis face,

bringing the Word to the hopeless proles
who've never had (and who won't have) souls,
    flighting in from Olympian blue
    to show them all a thing or two,

and for the girls with the better looks
he's quite prepared to sign his books
    (refined slim volume or weighty tome);
    he'll read and read till the cows come home,

86

mind and attention flag and drop
but he won't ever want to stop.
    He knows that what he calls his 'work'
    shines bright as stars in the general murk.

The rhetoric that the Poet brings
is far above terrestrial things,
    booming with symbols, myths and signs,
    improving Nature's dull designs.

As well as genius, he may be high
on several glasses of rum or rye –
    but that inspiring drunkard's slur
    is the genuine, true Impressionist blur

that shows contempt for the mean exact
of men who are timid and talk with 'tact'.
    And, later, when they gather round
    to say 'How lovely!' and 'How profound!'

and some confess themselves nonplussed
and 'influences' are discussed
    and 'Which living poets do you admire?'
    he warms himself, as at a fire,

among the Englit this and that,
and stretches and purrs like a basking cat –
    and winks a conspiratorial eye
    at the naked Muse in the English sky.

Strange how Potent Cheap Music is! *

When I began to care,
movies with Fred Astaire
could soften both the heartache and the shock;
romantic public song
could right my private wrong,
a healing and permissive Dr Spock.

For love (sex isn't meant)
is always slightly bent
and never seems to go quite straight ahead –
if Venus were the boss
we all should suffer loss
and end up very firmly in the red.

In those days She could croon
a simple woozy tune,
and this confirmed us in our feeling that
LOVE was the only thing,
long as a piece of string,
inscrutable, indefinable Cheshire Cat.

And even now, though rogue
ballads are not in vogue,
a few can still be found there in the charts.
It's a relief to sing
this, that or anything –
in pop the trumps are very often hearts.

Most people like a beat,
the musical élite
cannot deny Beethoven's cosmic thump –
Stravinsky too (I guess)
liked rhythm more than less,
and with their works the joint will really jump.

* Noël Coward (*Private Lives*)

So, music (highbrow, low)!
Like water let it flow!
Strong feeling is remembered in those notes,
a sad and sexy past
made bitter-sweet at last;
let Venus Polyhymnia have your votes!

Literary, Residential

Neurotic ladies
who go on courses
are often unable
to hold their horses.

Disturbed Humpty-Dumpties
of spite and fear,
it's not long before
the cracks appear.

They sit there like
a witch's curse
and giggle when rivals
read their verse.

Asked an opinion
(the foolish may),
'I think it's terrible!'
they'll say.

As alcoholics
like seeing double,
what they like is
causing trouble.

Disrupters from
the neat front parlour,
they're lonely/sad
like the tunes in Mahler.

You can't help them
(their poems might)
on their long, long journey
into night.

On the Menu

Coming very shortly are the following:
my wonderful cricket story *The Nattrass Overthrow*,
praised by all the critics as the best short novel
this century about a freak run-out;
Confessions Of A Muffdiver, flash autobiography
('I always loved that soft warm wetness with the fuzzy
    surround!'), banned and enjoyed
by everybody, a piece of smart revelation;
Did They Go Back To Felixstowe?, an Edwardian saga
trolloping through the Home Counties, full of fake
    history
and semi-under-housemaids, hierarchical,
fit to induce a television coma, with marvellous dialogue
like 'Goodbye, darling!' and 'So you both saw fit to . . .'
a winner of the Booker, apotheosis of the bogus.
All these are coming. But I shall sit at home
and write unacceptable epigrams about the status quo.

A Newly Discovered Poem, Written by Mr William Wordsworth in his Madness

It is some Book of Famous Fidgets
That He holds within His digits.
Some Tract that transcendental grows
Is what He traces with His toes.

Huge He is and looks quite weird
With His grey almighty Beard,
And there's something truly frightening
In the way He throws out lightning.

As He sits upon those Hills
Where we like sheep digest our Ills,
He is Lord of Place and Time –
The Egotistical Sublime!

Marry a Lord!

Saw a well-dressed woman on a train –
she was going to London for personal gain.
She was going to:
> dramatize her drawers,
> popularize her panties,
> make notable her knickers!

It was plain
she was on the make –
and no mistake!

I knew she was going to:
> marry a Lord –
> then marry another Lord –
> and then marry another Lord –
and get as much alimony
as they could afford!
With her low cunning
and her loving arts
and the private enterprise of her private parts!

I knew she was going to:
> marry a Lord –
> then marry another Lord –
> and then marry another Lord –

I knew they'd be bamboozled
but never (never) bored!
Breaking up homes
and breaking hearts
by the private enterprise of her private parts!

I knew by instinct,
without rhyme or reason,
she was heading for
the mating season!
I knew what she wanted,
what she had in mind –
and what she wanted
she would surely find!

I knew she was going to:
                marry a Lord –
                then marry another Lord –
                and then marry another Lord –
They'd all worship her,
she couldn't be ignored!
With her great beauty
and Cupid's darts
and the private enterprise of her private parts!

Miss God

My dear, of course it's a sin. All we can hope for is that
Miss God will forgive us. – W.H. Auden to Chester
Kallman

The sex-lives of the poets!
And Miss God flounces in!
Who cohabits and who coits
And with what sense of Sin –
This is her one big worry
And can't be worked out in a dreadful hurry.

In good moods she excuses
And turns a smiling face,
It's okay if it amuses –
She likes a bit of lace
And (an unmarried mother)
She's partial to a little of the other.

Often, when she is shaving,
She thinks 'Am I a *man*?'
(The angels would be raving)
But, flirting with a fan,
She ogles her creation –
And knows it's good, monogamy to masturbation.

The Meeting

In the long and boring meeting,
in the hot and boring meeting,
there was shouting by the Chairman,
bullying almost by the Chairman,
people rose on points of order,
caused chaos with points of order,
argument became emotive,
all the words used were emotive,
and this was the obvious reason
passion overcame all reason.

Everything was twice repeated,
sometimes more than twice repeated,
as they worked through the agenda
(it seemed elastic, that agenda,
becoming longer, never shorter),
their utterances grew long, not shorter,
it was just like spreading butter,
words went further, like spread butter,
covering each subject thinly,
covering almost nothing thinly.

People talked about resigning,
disgruntled talk was of resigning,
accusations in a covey
flew like partridge in a covey,
yet this was not entertaining –
it sounds like drama, entertaining
as the TV scenes in courtrooms –
this was *not* like scenes in courtrooms,
it contrived to be quite boring,
really quite immensely boring.

It was more like scenes where children
shout insults at other children,
it was like a verbal punch-up,
more long-winded than a punch-up,
but the bitterness and anger
brought out words like knives in anger,
it was more like verbal murder
if there's boredom in a murder –
any moderate survivors
in the end *felt* like survivors.

Like being rescued from a snowstorm,
or blinding words whirled like a snowstorm;
they could only cry for brandy,
go to pubs and order brandy,
they felt they deserved some medals
like the Army's campaign medals –
through the tumult and the shouting
(quiet was strange after the shouting)
they achieved the peace of something
through the meeting – which was something.

It was like peace after beating
heads on walls, like hours of beating
heads on walls and never stopping –
till at last the joy of stopping
seemed a truly great achievement,
lack of pain, a great achievement,
it's so lovely when you stop it!
Negative delight, to stop it,
flooded through them after meeting
at that long hot boring meeting!

A Coy Maiden Solicits Aid from a Critic

Porter, published Porter,
hear my plea,
be a big help to
little me!
Bring me succour
and bring me aid,
help me to call a
spade a spade,
make my adjectives
fit and apt,
you're an enthraller,
I am wrapt!
Take what's archaic
from my verse,
make it better –
at least not worse –
what's inverted
turn around,
save me from the
Liverpool Sound!

Porter, published Porter,
wave your wand,
get me out of
my Slough of Despond!
Make my rhymes for
ever true,
all my metaphors
sparkling new,
get metaphysics
into my lines,
I want fresh grapes
on my old vines
but I'd be glad if
you could stop
my love songs sounding
like last year's Pop –
not like a tatty
overblown tart,
I'd like you to make them
into Art.

A Ballad of the Good Lord Baden-Powell

(Companion Piece to Lawrence Durrell's *Ballad Of The Good Lord Nelson*)

If Lord Baden-Powell ever had a stand,
sex in the head or sex in the hand,
he fixed his mind on Matabeleland
      (till he pumped it all into a Lady)

He hadn't heard about white slave trafficking,
the only relief he had was Mafeking,
he liked war and the crying and havocking
      (till he jumped it all into a Lady)

He was a virgin who married late,
he told all the lads not to masturbate,
of blindness and madness this could create
    (till he bumped it all into a Lady)

In *Scouting For Boys* he clearly said
if temptation raises its ugly head
don't sleep in too warm or soft a bed
    (till he lumped it all into a Lady)

Never, he said, play fast and loose
with the pure male fluid, it's a vital juice –
cold baths will save you from self-abuse
    (till he flumped it all into a Lady)

On Brownsea Island the first Boy Scouts
were quite as green as Brussels Sprouts
and tied in knots by love's ins and outs
    (yes, he humped it all into a Lady)

But Puritans marry and fall in love,
Venus can coo like a well-born dove
and love is below as well as above
    (how he clumped it all into a Lady!)

When he wrote *Rovering To Success*
he'd seen a woman without a dress –
which once he would have thought sheer wickedness
    (and he rumped it all into a Lady)

So now his Gospel for ever abides,
proof against changing times and tides,
it's plainly written: *Boy scouts, girl guides*
    (wow! he dumped it all into a Lady!)

A Victorian Enigma

It was indeed an impenetrable type of being. A thick
growth of what a trichologist would have called hair
adorned the portion that might be described as the head;
and this was attached by a tubular structure consisting of
bone, musculature and other medical matter, covered in
skin, to what in some of our more popular murder cases
is inevitably headlined as the torso. From this depended
or protruded two upper limbs, having prehensile
attachments, while to the lower part of the body were
attached two longer and as it were smoothly extruded
features, used as supports during locomotion. The
attachments to these were almost completely lacking in
the prehensile quality above-mentioned.

From the front of the upper part of the body projected
two large soft protuberances, centred on which, as the
bull's eye on a target, two pink excrescences could be
seen. It was not hard to determine that the tissue of which
these last were constructed was of an erectile nature.

As the head boasted two adornments that might be
said to be eyes, one olfactory organ, and movable
mouth-parts, so the torso could be described as 'adorned'
by a pink and mouth-like generative organ (as we later
discovered it to be), situated between the two lower
limbs. To this, indeed, a crisp overgrowth of
comparatively short hairs added an air of importance –
and even of mystery.

The creature seemed, as we gathered round to inspect
it more closely, almost oblivious of our scrutiny. We
learned later that it was in all probability silently
contemplating its own uniqueness; the eyes had a
far-away look, and one of the prehensile attachments to
an upper limb was partly inserted in the organ situated at
the junction of the legs, which it gently agitated with a
mild strumming motion.

Both Professor Doyle and Mr Wells were transported by their contemplation of this primitive organism. 'Only to think,' cried Professor Doyle in tones of rapture, 'that I should be privileged to see with my own eyes this prehistoric phenomenon, known to us hitherto only from the writings of the Greek and Roman poets and philosophers!'

Stripping a Teenage Wall

This wall is a palimpsest,
a parchment written on twice
(under the shirt lies the vest).
Images – nasty, nice –

have been cut out, Copydexed,
some in the name of Tesco
commercially oversexed
and some Old Masters, fresco

and easel painting, photos
that once appealed to my daughter.
Offered to Art, ex-votos
and lambs to the slaughter,

clipped from the Supplement page –
like the temples of Mayas
they remind of an earlier age.
I descend through the layers.

Beneath Michelangelo's 'Night'
a priceless Korky The Cat
and Minnie Mouse, black and white,
under some four-colour tat

advertising a wine,
all evening-dress slinky.
Days when Mick Jagger seemed fine
and Rupert Bear kinky!

Sophisticated! Joined hands
of a Florentine martyr
cover the rollicking bands
(geological strata)

of the pre-teen comic strips
where the nippers are nipping
in a child's world without hips
or strippers stripping.

Using a thing like an adze
I peel them away from the wall –
a young woman's fashions and fads,
innocent Eve and the Fall.

My Children's Book

So I sit down and create a few characters:
a horrible rabbit called Big Bunny Biscuits,
who tortures little children by means of arithmetic,
snapping off their arms and legs when they can't add up;
a buccaneering dog called Billy Barker,
whose terrifying growl makes little girls deaf
at a range of half a mile; a sinister sheep
who treats little boys' heads as pasture
and crops them down to a velvety crewcut.
Its name is Capillary Phlogiston.

All babies, at birth, are forcibly inducted
into the Anti-Saccharine Society.
In the Great Jungle are child-eating orchids
(Rhodesia-Boysonia); there are world-beating snakes
and a very bad pop group called *Chrys an' the mums*.

In my book even the jokes will be bad.
Everyone will live in a state of disgrace
and have misadventures. No angels or fairies
will be able to stand the atmosphere for more than a
    minute.
Real life (of any kind) will seem a blessed relief.

Burlesque: Auden in the Forties

Deftly, admiral, from your fly
    Draw the huge unwilling cock,
Let unlettered lovers sigh,
    Love can fade and time can mock,
But you are Venus' prey
    From head to toe
And twice as gay
        As any well-hung, bell-bottomed
        Matelot.

'Hello, sailor!' is the cry
    History greets you with in bars,
The pink cadets scream 'Me, oh My!'
    While mad Furies in fast cars
Drive past but not away,
        Whatever you
May think or say,
        They're ready, hell or high water,
        To pursue.

Barbarians drink castles dry,
    Darlings live and die in bed,
All our futures are a lie,
    Truth invests the past instead:
Pretty blossoms on the may,
        Louche blackbirds urge
You not to stay –
        The fateful poem, well-written,
        Is a dirge.

The Ballad of Erse O. Reilly

(A Nonsense Of Ireland)

Oh, sure ye'll have heard of that witwandering scholar
that was in for a penny and in for a pound and in for an
    almighty dollar
how he opened the eyes of the foculties with his don's
    donnees like valerian
antispasmodic and clumping about with his bad rhymes
    like a megatherium

> *Chorus* Jim McJoyce's silly sanitarium
>   full of delirium!

He was the boyo for all the accredited academicals
Arragh! they tested every sinful syllable with their
    syllabub syllabus chemicals
but he wron away from them still catcalling teasily
Let the rabbit see the stoat! They were woeful and weaselly.

> *Chorus* He sang breezily
>   *Hell Comes Easily!*

For the Muse had him by the horn and no Englit sanitary
    Deportment
could prise them apart, it was synthetic and a seamless
    garment
she let him feel the weight of her Titfield Thunderbolts
    surely
it was a game with spatial rules, it was educated hurley

> *Chorus* Short and curly
>   she loved him dearly.

So they never gat him, though they brought in a true bill
    of damages
and put a spectral scanner onto his sob-standard
    Skandiknavian languages
He was one too much for them, in Cameforth,
    Oxbritches and Iowa
they never neutered his nastiness with Festicles of Light
    at Rhayader

Chorus Take a short ride on her
with a girl guide on her.

Homage Comforts Exiles. He sang like an aviary.
This is his Celtic abbreviated breviary.

For the Ghost of Nancy Mitford

Hear the haughty highborn ladies,
dancing through their marble halls,
lovely in their silks and satins,
gay from evensong to matins –
talking balls.

Hear the sporting shooting ladies
crossing moors of grouse and rock,
much preferring hares and pheasants
to the humble local peasants –
talking cock.

Hear the gambling bosomed beauties,
chips in each delicious lap,
full of cognac, gin and vinos,
when dice roll in rich casinos –
talking crap.

They Flee from Me
That Sometime Did Me Seek

At this moment in time
the chicks that went for me
in a big way
are opting out;
as of now, it's an all-change situation.

The scenario was once,
for me, 100% better.
Kissing her was viable
in a nude or semi-nude situation.
It was *How's about it, baby?*,
her embraces were relevant
and life-enhancing.

I was not hallucinating.
But with regard to that one
my permissiveness
has landed me in a forsaking situation.
The affair is no longer on-going.
She can, as of now, explore new parameters –
How's about it? indeed!
I feel emotionally underprivileged.
What a bitch!
(and that's meaningful!).

Dialogue Between the Alcoholic and his Better Self

A   Would you like a gin and tonic?
B   No, I'd rather have bubonic

                              plague!

A   Try a Haig

    or a dark and sexy Guinness?
    Your idea of getting thin is

                              out.

B   Please, no stout!

A   Are you partial to a lager,
    as Slavonic as a saga?
B   No!
    Donne-moi de l'eau!

A Why not have an iced Campari?
    It's as basic as a Maori
                        dance.
B Not a chance!

A Many people fancy ouzo
    as Man Friday fancied Crusoe.
B   Greek?
    Not this week!

A Try the calming glass of claret
    that the poet in a garret
                    · sipped.
B Man, you've flipped!

A Could you down a pint of bitter?
B Please excuse me if I titter!
                      Ale
    in the Holy Grail

    wouldn't tempt me – nor would cider!
    I'm quite fly (though you're a spider).
                         Tea
    is for me!

A Frisky whisky, sherry, brandy
    can contribute to a randy
                    lay.
B GO AWAY!
    You have plenitude and foison
    of these drinks, the purest poison
                      known –
    leave me alone!

    I'll turn cartwheels when you've gone, the
    truth is I'm happy on the
                    shelf.
    Drink them yourself!

A Male Chauvinist Celebrates International Women's Year *

It's been a particularly good year
for women
(I should like to raise a true connoisseur's cheer
for women),
a Vintage Year – 1975 –
and women can make one glad to be alive.

They've all matured particularly well
in the hot sun,
developing good contours, skin colour and smell
in the hot sun –
they're at their very best with music and wine.
Try one tonight. You can have one of mine.

* This poem was a winner of a *New Statesman* competition.

Asked to Write a Poem on the Subject 'Who Am I?' by the Magazine Nova, 1975

Once I was an ovum, and At Home to a sperm.
Soon I wore a prep school cap for term after term.
For most of my twenties I was busy with a War,
in a mud-coloured uniform I didn't much adore.

Then I worked in agencies, in a dark office suit,
at ads too full of adjectives, much fruitier than fruit,
copywriting. After that I was a freelance next,
shabby in my casual clothes, a plain straightforward text.

'Role-playing' is the word they use; and one certainly can
think of more than Shakespeare's seven ages of man –
the baby, the bully, the boyfriend and the bore
are simply variants of the apple, all with the same core?

106

There's a cupboardful of costumes – what would I want
   to be?
What would I like the world to think the quintessential
   me?
Anthologize! The best of each unsatisfactory stage
might make a compound flattering to me in my old age.

The teenage vigour, as it were, the bright and youthful
   looks
could be combined with wisdom (gained from reading
   all those books).
Oh, so clever and attractive! That's man's (and woman's)
   wish,
who in the womb once had the nature of a fish.

Human beings' pretensions are the braying of an ass,
It's right our dissolution causes, mainly, gas;
and our feeling so important doesn't, either, get us far –
for a vast amount of nothing is what we really are.

The Germanic Day

I wake the wifehag in the marriagebed
She makes quickcoffee in the breakfastcups
We wake the girlchild in her sleepingroom
I take the hounddog for a pavementwalk
We eat the cornflakes and the baconegg

I drive the smallcar to the officeblock
I read the newmail on the clear desktop
My giggling girlclerk takes the shorthand down
Reports from salesmen take up workingtime
My brainpan rings with what the farsound says

I mealeat in Directors' Diningroom
The Chairman tells me of his own forecast
The afternoon has salesfigures for food
Salesareas talk in the meetingroom
A wellshaped lovegirl brings the teacups in

I end the workday with campaignplan talk
My girlclerk tells of farcalls from outside
I drive the smallcar to the privatehouse
I take the hounddog for a pavementwalk
I kiss the wifehag in the marriagebed.

Rooms Must be Vacated Before Noon on Day of Departure

At the end of an Irish tour, in a town that could be called
Trevorstown after William Trevor, who lived here
before he changed his name and became a famous
novelist and lived in Devonshire, a town whose name
some of the natives of the country pronounce as though

it were the sound made by an English crow –

but I pronounce it like the name of the thing that gets
stuck in the neck of a bottle – in the Glenvera I enjoy a
sausage-egg-and-tea delicious breakfast, modifying thus
the slight hangover induced by mixing St Raphael with
Cork Dry Gin,

and I have almost no sense of sin.

Why should I? Literary tours and excursions are
meritorious endeavours and those who engage in them
deserve well of the creature comforts and should never
creep about crying *Peccavi!*, as they rattle in trains across
the centre of Ireland, which is very flat –

but that's enough of that.

I don't want to talk about guilt and I won't talk about
guilt because this, although it is work of a kind, is also a
kind of holiday and I have a sense of release drinking
Guinness in Montenotte – where the sun shines down in
a very Italianate way

and work seems very like play.

108

For Patience Strong

A wife is like a court jester (but without a sense of
humour); she's there to make a grape fruit feel like a
satsuma – to cut her husband down to size, to make him
feel small, or as though (like Hitler) he had only one ball.
A monorch, not a monarch, and by no means a king, and
not really very much good at anything. This is the course
of action that a wife pursues, when she's not moaning
low or singing the blues. There's not a lot that a husband
can do, although in so many cases this is true, and success
may not crown even a determined attempt – because, as
well as children, familiarity breeds contempt.

Gritty

(A Subaltern's True Story, 1942)

Driving a tractor towing a Bofors gun
in the early morning (ice on the road?)
Gunner Gritty slid into a tree.

Crushed in his cab in that cold winter sun,
he later died, 'shedding his earthly load'
the Padre might have said. To me

(a junior subaltern), the BSM,
the man of God, there fell the routine task:
to represent the unit at his grave

up in North London, London's suburb hem,
and, duty done, what more could we three ask
than the deserved pub lunch? Alcohol gave

comfort, food warmed our thoughts of pity.
The Sergeant-Major, quite seriously, said to me:
'I shouldn't have the pudding if I were you, Sir.
It's gritty.'

PART FOUR

Crucifixion

Suppose they came along one morning and said 'Right! To-day we're going to crucify you!' It would come as a shock, to say the least; and particularly if they had already set up a brand new wooden cross, handmade, in your back garden, and had the hammers and high quality nails ready, no expense spared, to do the thing in style. After the first numbness of the shock, who would be able to resist shouting and screaming, completely hysterical or even technically mad? There would certainly be fainting and falling about. We forget too easily how such cruelty was once commonplace, no more regarded than (nowadays) a starving lost dog in the harsh streets of a big city. The man or woman who could contemplate the endurance of such torture – for they would not hesitate to crucify women, and even children – with the calm and philosophical courage advised by the Ancients would be rare indeed.

Dirty Weekends

Dirty weekends. Something so soiled, snide, sly and now (Venus be praised!) so old-fashioned about these words; from the days of frustration, puritanism and secret meetings. Faked hotel registers and a general feeling of dirty knickers and used French letters. And yet such encounters and companionships can be as full of true love (in the baleful words of the song-writers) as the arranged and church marriages that reoccur in photographic colour in photographers' shops in provincial towns; He and She both decked and smiling, the little bouquet of bad-taste bridesmaids, a tortured god in the background. For what is touched and what is felt, in both cases – the union for two days or for a lifetime – is not pink flesh only; the emotions too are engaged. Those erections that cause sniggering among schoolboys and schoolgirls are spiritual things. The nipples, to the lover, are not just utilitarian and of the laity, but holy. The girl shines in the dark like an angel or the Virgin Mary, and the word 'worship' is not in the church service only, but in reality.

Romeo Addresses his Poperin Pear

You've been inside Juliet, you lucky little thing! You've been part, temporarily, of an extraordinarily beautiful person. When we were together, you belonged to her and she belonged to me. Although my wise uncles say that no person can or should 'belong' to another person; and in a love like ours, where everything is freely given, there is no question of one being the property of the other. My wise uncles also say that, just as most men do regard their wives as their property, a large number of girls regard a boyfriend as a personal possession and wives, even more so, regard their husbands as belonging to them like a carved chest or an embroidery frame.

You look, now, so coy and bashful. So innocent, so incapable of that brazen effrontery, that stiff resistance in the face of love, that ardour in the armed encounter! And yet you know a thing or two, an adept in the mysteries of women, designed to tear the veil of the temple and penetrate to the holy of holies, the Grail, the womb, that tidebound inward sea. . . .

How could this lamb be so like a lion, so rampageous, so rampant, storming the ramparts, effecting a breach, received in the citadel with joy, a relieving army?

You are indeed a two-face, both shy and shocking, in your two wildly different moods. I'm watching you, you cyclothyme! Juliet is watching you too. She has a small smile on her face and she is sending you a message of congratulation: 'Well done, my good and faithful servant!'

Love Difficulties

In my time the whores have said to me encouraging whorelike things – such as 'You're putting on weight!' and 'Nice and hard!' – while women engaged in it more for love than money have remarked 'You underestimate yourself' and 'That looks to me remarkably like an erection'. But never (and for this kindness I shall always be grateful) when there was impotence or difficulty did any of them taunt me with the contemptuous insults that young men so much fear: 'You're not a man!', 'Tie a pencil to it!' etc. etc.

It's too easy to equate sexual performance with masculinity. Not lack of maleness but the fixating mothers and the castrating fathers are to blame. Many thoroughgoing homosexuals are able (I mean the male ones) to have intercourse with women – but they're not much interested in it. On the other hand, men who love women are more likely to be afraid of failure; and even perhaps because of their anxiety to do well, to lose potency for that very reason. Specific anxiety over the outcome is allied to the oedipal fears and guilts.

From all such depressing sadnesses, may Venus deliver us!

A Glastonbury Cricket Match

Frottie Fridges was the next person in, the very last person to bat for the Wookey Hole cricket team. Frottie Fridges was a complete and perfect rhombus, with the look of a squeezed square. Nature had made her four feet high and not very much thicker, reckoned from back to front, than the big front door at the Vicarage. In her pads and batting gloves this mammalian repository of local wisdom had indeed the appearance of a very wide deformed cricket bat herself.

As she approached the wicket her shrewd Quantock brain was occupied with intense rustic thoughts, concerning for the most part the Vicar and his lover, the beautiful Nuttie Zetland. She was thinking, as she took guard: 'He do masturbate she, and she do masturbate he. But 'tis a girt mock to reason how none o' these wold sinners do never masturbate *me*!'

So saying and thinking, with great female complacency, she settled down to await the next ball of the over. Meanwhile all the blades of grass on the cricket pitch were striving with a kind of communistic solidarity, to take a decisive part in the game. They were at one with the thirteen players exercising themselves there, and far more deeply engaged than the two umpires. As the ball struck them they did their very best to divert it towards the wicket, since all pitches do their utmost to assist the bowler.

Mad Lekker, as he walked slowly back before turning to bowl again, sniffed viciously as he passed Nuttie, who was the batswoman at the other end. His little bear's eyes narrowed as they rested on her classic breasts. Imaginative lust carried him forward, flooding into the remotest portion of his consciousness. He became a wave in the Bristol Channel, a crystal in a Mendip stone wall, a black-striped perch in the Brue under Pomparles Bridge. On his right as he walked, dogsplurge burgeoned and the

114

ratsfoot spread its purple patches evenly over the outfield, awaking in him atavistic affiliations. On his left the vivid green of the cat's crocus attracted his wandering gaze as he turned on his heel and hesitated, 'alone and palely loitering', before beginning his run-up to bowl. Only slightly distracted now by Nuttie Zetland's perfect breasts, in their rough cheesecloth cricket shirt, he broke wind and began to gallop towards the crease. The dark earth beneath him seemed to him then, under its covering of grass, like a vast wild-maned horse, upon whose back he was being borne through space! A poignant smell of musk rose up from where his heavy white boots pressed against that huge living creature. From that fragment of white mystery there slid across land and water into the soul of Mad, as he approached and passed Nuttie's earthy presence and released the leather sphere, the curt voice of the umpire, Lord M.'s bastard: 'No ball!'

> – J.C. Powys, Captain
> Somerset Second XI, 1933